CALIFORNIA

Designed and Produced by

Ted Smart & David Gibbon

MAYFLOWER BOOKS · NEW YORK CITY

EVER since one wet January day in 1884 when a carpenter at John A. Sutter's Sawmill picked up a chunk of yellow metal and started one of history's great gold rushes, California has been to many the promised land; a land of unlimited opportunity.

People flocked to California in search of gold; they piled onto the railroads when the lines were first pushed into California; they walked, drove and hitched into California when the citrus and grape industries called out for labor, when oil and natural gas were discovered, when Hollywood promised overnight stardom, when drought turned huge areas of the American southwest into a Dust Bowl, when shipyards and aircraft plants opened up thousands of new jobs.

In 1848 the population was estimated at 14,000; by the 1860s it was well on the way to half a million and between 1860 and 1960 it doubled virtually every 20 years. California has long since overtaken New York as the most heavily populated member of the United States and is now approaching a figure of 20 million – roughly one in 20 of all Americans. By the year 2000 population pundits believe that that figure will have become one in five.

With this tremendous surge of manpower has come immense industrial muscle which, allied to the academic, artistic, scientific and commercial expertise attracted from around the world by unrivaled salaries and unsurpassed working conditions, has propelled California into a unique position: only five nations of the world produce and sell more goods than does this one American state, and one of those nations is the United States itself.

"California", says Michael Davie in his book, *In the Future Now*,* "is the only society ever founded on respect for money, which is one reason why it is now the richest segment of the surface of the globe, and why Californians are the richest people there have ever been."

But even with the strength of its people, even with their highly successful "Work hard, play hard" philosophy, it is doubtful if California would have made such a mark on the world, or such wealth for its citizens, without its abundant natural attributes.

Its magnificent climate is certainly one. The coastal strip – roughly 2 percent of the State and where 94 percent of the people live – luxuriates in temperatures that rarely exceed 90 degrees F (32 degrees C) or fall to freezing point. Rainfall is moderate, about 20 inches a year in San Francisco, for instance. Yet north of that city there are areas that are deluged by as much as 180 inches a year. In the far south, summer temperatures in the desert areas hit Sahara heights, while the peaks of the Sierra Nevadas often experience temperatures as low as those of the Arctic.

The state's 158,000 square miles contain the impressive mountain ranges of the Sierra Nevada, as well as forests, deserts, lakes and 1,200 miles of the most beautiful coastal scenery to be seen anywhere, now protected by the extensive powers of a specially appointed Coastal Commission.

Within less than 100 miles of each other in California lie the highest and lowest points of mainland USA – Mt Whitney at 14,494 feet, and Death Valley, 282 feet below sea level at it lowest point. The Valley was known to

*Hamish Hamilton, London, 1972

Red Indian tribes for generations, but was unknown to white man until a party of prospectors seeking a shortcut to the gold fields stumbled upon it. It is now a national monument.

Mt Whitney is part of the Sierra Nevada range that runs south for 430 miles from Lassen Peak to the fringes of Los Angeles. It is quite an experience for the first-time visitor to Los Angeles to drive along Melrose Avenue in a temperature of 80 degrees F or more, while the snow capped peaks of the Sierras glint a dazzling white in the summer sky to the north.

High up in the Sierras, near the state border with Nevada, is one of the most beautiful of America's lakes, Lake Tahoe, more than 6,000 feet above sea level, nearly 200 square miles in area and, at a depth of 1,600 feet, one of the world's deepest. It is now a superbly developed resort area with Olympic standard skiing facilities, casinos, cabarets and nightclubs where the finest of America's entertainers regularly appear.

The state's main desert areas are the Colorado in the south west where fewer than three inches of rain fall in a year and some of the world's highest temperatures have been recorded and the Mojave Desert, where apart from a few military installations, aviation and rocket ranges and the occasional intrepid explorer, the desert's 25,000 square miles are as unsullied by human endeavor as on the day they were created (although efforts were made recently to establish a nuclear power plant there!).

California's forests, however, *have* suffered from the arrival of the settler. The redwood forests, for instance, where many of these magnificent trees are up to 2,000 years old and tower 300 feet, now cover less than 10 percent of their former territory. Recent, far-reaching state legislation ensures there will be no further inroads into one of California's great legacies.

The arrival of settlers, and the inevitable erosion of some of the state's natural beauty and riches, dates from the discovery of gold. But California's history, as far as the white man is concerned, goes back another century. The Spaniards can claim to have discovered California – then occupied by scattered Red Indian tribes – and by the late 18th century Franciscan friars were establishing missions along the Pacific coasts, the first at San Diego in 1769. The Spaniards were eventually ousted by the Mexicans, leaving behind little more than their architecture and place names. In 1846, the emergent United States defeated Mexico and huge tracts of land, including much of modern California, became American, and in 1850 California became the 31st state of the Union.

At this time, of course, gold was still the major preoccupation of the State's immigrants; it had lured them into San Francisco by boat from all over Europe, as well as in more than 6,000 wagons on the hazardous overland trail from the Midwest and the east, where cholera claimed more victims than hostile Indian tribes or extremes of climate and terrain.

Chinese faces became increasingly seen among the predominantly Anglo-Saxon workers and they stayed to form the origins of the Chinese communities in California today. Fifteen years later the railroads were dynamiting through the Rockies with the aid of hundreds of Irish laborers who also stayed on and, with the Italians and French, made San Francisco their new home.

The city had been founded only a century before, in 1776 when a landing was made in the Bay by a Spanish expedition. Until California entered the Union, San Francisco was little more than a Spanish settlement, but in the 1830s the first American homes and ranches were established on the slopes of the 43 hills. With the Gold Rush all that changed, and the Bay suddenly had to cope with vessels arriving daily from all parts. Wharves were hastily erected to cope with them; the hillsides suddenly sprouted tents and shanties, and the shrewder settlers opened up bars and gambling houses to part the prospectors from their golden gains.

Within ten years of the first find, San Francisco's 1845 population of about 300 had swelled to nearly 60,000, and the city had already established a character of its own. There was a Chinatown; North Beach was where the Italians set up home, and the Barbary Coast provided nightlife. There was also a commercial center and the peripheral services needed for the life style spawned by the Gold Rush.

In the 1860s, oil replaced gold as the Californian bonanza and, until the end of the century, San Francisco's population and city development expanded fast. Then, in the course of a few minutes early on the morning of April 18, 1906, life as San Francisco knew it came to an end. An initial two-minute earthquake tremor bowled over buildings and sparked off fires that raged for three days across the city, killing more than 500 and, by destroying nearly 30,000 buildings, virtually razed the whole of the city's development.

As with the Great Fire of London, however, the disaster gave the City Fathers an opportunity to stamp out the unhygienic, cramped conditions caused by hasty, unplanned building and to reconstruct on far more generous lines. In less than 10 years the new San Francisco took shape, celebrated in 1915 by the Panama-Pacific Exposition.

As the 20th century progressed, the city's fine natural harbor ensured it became a major shipbuilder, mainly of naval craft, and many who came to work in the shipyards and allied industries as part of the war effort stayed on in San Francisco. Another expansion in population occurred after the opening in 1936 of the Oakland Bay Bridge, the eight and a quarter miles of which make it the longest steel bridge in the world. With two levels of traffic (replacing the ferry boat system across the Bay) it opened up the East Bay area into a major dormitory suburb of the city. More expansion followed in the 1960s with such elegant developments as the Golden Gateway and Ghirardelli Square near Fisherman's Wharf, one of the highlights of most visitors' itinerary.

San Franciscans like to think, with some justice, that their city provides a cultural oasis in the Californian social desert. Its museums include four devoted to the fine arts; Golden Gate Park houses the California Academy of Sciences; and specialist museums include wine, army and maritime exhibits, as well as institutions of local history such as Cable Bar Barn, the old U.S. Mint, and the Wells Fargo History Room.

It has its own symphony orchestra, opera and ballet companies, and a wide range of more contemporary music – jazz, ragtime and rock. And the many excellent ethnic restaurants reflect the cosmopolitan character of the city.

For 60 years San Francisco was the major Californian city but by the 1920s it was being overtaken in size, and significance to the state economy, by its brash southern counterpart: Los Angeles. With around three million people, L.A. – as it is universally known – now has about four times the population of San Francisco. It was proclaimed by Father Crespi in 1769 when he accompanied the Spanish Expeditionary Force, led by Gaspar de Portola. The first mission, San Gabriel, was founded there in 1771 and with the addition of another, San Fernando, the resulting settlement grew large enough to be considered the chief town of Mexican California.

The Gold Rush to the north altered the town's development and it became a rowdy cattle town until the Santa Fe railroad brought in arrivals, many of them farmers from the Midwest who exploited the rich farming region. Within the five years or so of the railroad's arrival in 1885, the orange-growing industry and the development of new towns around the central Los Angeles area saw the population increase to 50,000. By the turn of the century, with the discovery of oil and the opening up of port facilities at San Pedro, the population had more than doubled.

Individual communities such as Anaheim, Glendale, Santa Monica and Beverly Hills were absorbed, first by the advent of the automobile then by further building development pulling them all together into one urban area, and with Hollywood established on the map, Los Angeles emerged as the State's major city.

There are conflicting stories about how Hollywood came to be named. None can be proved, but one that seems as likely as any other is that an early English settler family trying to recreate a little of their origins, planted holly trees in their garden. The climate put an end to the holly wood, but the name lived on.

Hollywood is now but an echo of the past. The film studios that remain are largely given over to television work. The area itself is a mosaic of office blocks, waste lots, hamburger stands, supermarkets, and second-class movie theaters. The domestic architecture is mock Spanish, mock Georgian, mock Gothic and mock Tyrolean and the inhabitants seem to spend most of their leisure hours hosing the carefully manicured lawns that run straight down to the sidewalks. As Edward Thorpe writes in his book, *The Other Hollywood,** "Glamorous Hollywood is just the receding architectural hairline of the thirties, a fading generation frozen in the forties and fifties, and the young kids of today in the tatty cast-offs of various fashionable folk lores. Topographically it is fast becoming just a no-man's land between the business areas of downtown Los Angeles and the swank and plush areas of Beverly Hills and Bel Air." Sad, but true.

Since World War II, the city has continued to prosper with leisure industries, aerospace, fashion and sport joining movies and TV as major employers and money earners for the city.

*Michael Joseph, London, 1970.

The Los Angeles Opera Company was founded in 1924, two years after the Hollywood Bowl was built for live outdoor performances of all kinds from symphony concerts, the Beatles and Bob Dylan to political rallies. The city's prestigious Music Center was built in the 1960s and the several art galleries include the Norton Simon and J. Paul Getty museums. There is the Museum of Science and Industry at Exposition Park and the Hall of Science and Travel in Griffith Park.

With the amazing Forest Lawn Memorial Cemetery in Glendale, whose Slumberland, Whispering Pines and replicas of the Wee Kirk o' the Heather and da Vinci's *Last Supper* were satirized in Waugh's *The Loved Ones,* and with Disneyland, the superb playground for children and adults at Anaheim, L.A. has two of America's best-known attractions.

Yet, despite their size and significance, neither Los Angeles nor San Francisco is the State capital. That honor belongs to Sacramento, the cradle of California, where Marshall, the carpenter at Sutter's Sawmill, picked up the state's future on that rainy day in 1884. Sacramento's Capitol Building, housing the State legislature, was built in 1861 and its archives and library hold in their files the enthralling and dramatic history of California.

When asked a few years ago what California had to offer, a state government official made the following points: an unmatched educational system allowing greater economic opportunity; newer buildings, therefore better houses and offices; and the best system of highways in the United States.

Educational facilities are almost unparalleled. The state pumps in well over 700 million dollars in funds to the educational system which, at the higher level, was hugely expanded in the 1960s. The existing University of California campuses at Berkeley (perhaps the most prestigious of them, founded 1868), Los Angeles, Davis, Riverside, Santa Barbara and San Francisco were supplemented by new sites at Irvine, Santa Cruz and San Diego. The California university system has produced many notable academics and is proud of the nearly 20 Nobel prize winners on its faculties. It houses two nuclear research laboratories, nearly 100 research and experimental stations and in many fields of endeavor – particularly medicine, science and biology – is in the forefront of world research.

As the state moved into the 1970s it had over 14 million registered vehicles, the greatest concentration in the world. To cope with this mobile army there were nearly 4,000 miles of multi-lane freeways and it was possible to drive north for 500 miles from San Diego on free motorways without having to stop for a traffic light or intersection.

California life as practiced, as eulogized in song and on film, is one of perpetual motion. The Californian moves home and travels in the course of business and pleasure far more than any other American. And in a city like Los Angeles, which covers such a huge area and in which public transport plays such a minor part, a car is absolutely essential.

But this brings its own problems. "By the early 1980s," Michael Davie reported one authority as saying, "we'll have 20 million cars. We've already got 14 million. I've got three myself: one for me, one for my wife, one for my son. It's out of control. You know they even want to put a freeway through one of the national parks…".

So, as California forges into the 1980s, the pioneer of new lifestyles, the voice of protest against rapid change is growing – against freeways, pollution, high technology and a multitude of other subjects. At risk, it says, is the very quality of life.

This growing feeling has spawned over the past decade a rash of cults and sects: theosophists, followers of Krishnamurti, Rosicrucians, the Beat Generation, Hippies, Zen Buddhists, creeds based on the occult, on faith healing, rock music, drugs and communes.

It is as if, after years of leading the world in experimentation, Californians are seeking to pause for breath, to take stock of their lives, to seek new solutions to new problems.

The State is aware of these feelings; almost every week there is legislative action of some kind dealing with energy, water, land use – all issues that have a major bearing on the quality of life.

And to ensure that the state does not forget its responsibilities, pressure groups – nearly 600 on the environment alone – are active on all the major issues, the chief of which is whether and how the land should be used or changed, and for whose benefit.

On their past record, Californians have the ability and the resources to deal with their problems; to move into a new era like the one that began 130 years ago at Sutter's Mill.

Highway 5, shown left, leads into San Diego, known as the 'birthplace of California'. San Diego Bay forms one of the world's great natural harbors and the city above, right and below *has grown up along the water's edge.*

Overleaf *is pictured the Charthouse Golf Course and the San Diego-Coronado Bay Bridge.*

The Star of India *above left, moored in San Diego harbor, is an authentic sailing ship that was originally launched in 1863.*

Coronado is situated on a peninsula which separates San Diego from the Pacific Ocean. It is an attractive resort in lovely surroundings and it provides excellent opportunities for outdoor pursuits of all kinds. Fishing below *is ever popular and golf may be enjoyed at the lovely Charthouse Course, featured* right *against a background of the San Diego–Coronado Bay Bridge.*

Boats rest at anchor in the Coronado Marina above *and the building* below left *is the Coronado Hotel, a popular venue for vacationers.*

Whales, seals, dolphins, sharks, exotic birds
and picturesque gardens are just some of the
attractions of Sea World, Mission Bay, San
Diego, a 40-acre marine life park that offers
entertainment for all ages.

One of the big – in more ways than one –
shows is that featuring Shamu, the killer
whale, shown left and below. This
magnificent, 3-ton creature performs an
amazing routine of leaps (up to 24 feet out of
the water), rolls, dives and spins during his
spectacular 'Shamu Goes to College' act.

Operated by the Zoological Society of San Diego, which also controls the San Diego Zoo, the San Diego Wild Animal Park is situated 30 miles northeast of the city.

The park contains a five-mile long, silent monorail system with a driver-guide who offers a commentary on many of the park's animals and their characteristics.

Among the many interesting exhibits to be found in the Wild Animal Park are: Nairobi Village, which features lush gardens filled with exotic and rare fauna, a recreation of an African Kraal, a tropical American rain forest, Gorilla Grotto, containing a family of lowland gorillas, a Kilimanjaro Hiking Trail which leads the visitor through 1¼ miles of simulated East African landscape and, of course, numerous shows, elephant rides, music from around the world, restaurants and picnic areas.

A visit to the San Diego Wild Animal Park can be a delight for all ages and is ideal for family outings.

The San Diego Wild Animal Park has gained worldwide acclaim for its animal conservation efforts. It contains over 3,000 animals roaming freely in habitats resembling, as far as possible, their native homelands.

In addition to the more usual animals, such as the giraffe, zebras, rhinoceros and sacred ibis featured on these pages, there are also more unusual species as well as musical entertainments featuring Bluegrass Concerts and Trinidad Calypso Steel Bands.

Balboa Park has been transformed, in a little over a hundred years, from a wilderness into a center of cultural and recreational facilities for San Diego. It now contains beautifully landscaped gardens, art galleries, museums, theaters, a golf course and the world's largest zoo. The park was chosen as the site for the Panama-California International Exposition, which was held in 1915 and 1916, after which it was given its present name. It was at this time that several of the beautiful exhibit halls were built in Spanish colonial style, including the lovely Casas del Prado top and bottom left, above right and below, *the California Tower* above, *and the Natural History Museum* center left.

Balboa Park was also the setting for another world's fair, the California-Pacific International Exposition, which was staged in 1935 and 1936, when new exhibit halls, comprising the Pan-American Plaza, were built.

The evening sky overleaf provides a perfect backdrop for the California Tower and some of the lush vegetation in Balboa Park.

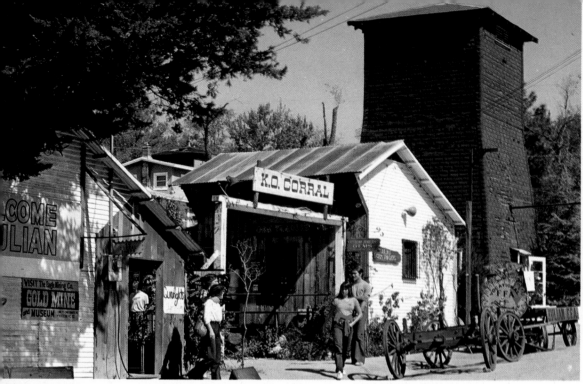

Julian pictured on this page *lies in San Diego's back country. A former gold mining town, Julian has been preserved very much as it was and it still retains the flavor of those heady, free-spending days. The old methods of panning for gold are still demonstrated and visitors may also try their hand, perhaps feeling a little of the excitement of 'gold-fever'.*

San Diego Old Town was the site of the original Mission San Diego de Alcala, which was eventually moved the few miles to its present location. Old Town contains 19 state historic landmarks and many of the old adobe buildings have been converted, and are now used as restaurants and shops.

Sherman Gilbert House overleaf left, in Old Town, was originally built in 1887. Known as the 'Mother of the Missions' and founded by Juniper Serra, Mission San Diego overleaf right stands timeless in the California sunshine.

Point Loma is a high promontory sheltering
San Diego Bay from the vast expanse of the
Pacific Ocean. It was here that Juan Cabrillo,
who is credited with the discovery of
California, landed his ship in 1542 and his
statue stands high on the point.

The old lighthouse left and center right on
top of Point Loma was erected in 1855. Its
light was frequently obscured by cloud,
however, and it was supplanted, in 1891, by
the present Coast Guard Lighthouse which
stands close to the water's edge.

The fig tree above at Moreton Bay provides
welcome shade from the hot sun.

Sunset above right at Mission Bay throws
into silhouette the shapes of the palm trees.

The spectacular Singing Hills Golf Club
pictured below right is located in El Cajon,
on the outskirts of San Diego, and the expanse
of water below comprises the Sutherland
Reservoir in the Cleveland National Forest.

The Pacific Ocean surges onto the shore at
San Diego overleaf left and Highway 78 is
shown overleaf right as it disappears into the
distance at Santa Ysabel.

Since the last century vacationers have enjoyed the pleasures that La Jolla, north of San Diego, pictured on these pages has to offer. All manner of seashore pursuits may be enjoyed on this lovely stretch of coastline.

La Jolla has its serious side, however, for it is here that the Scripps Institution of Oceanography and the Salk Institute for Biological Studies carry out much of their valuable research. Just off the coast of La Jolla lies Scripps Canyon, one of the most extensively studied of all submarine canyons, named because of its nearness to the Institution.

The shimmering, beautifully colored and marked peacock overleaf was photographed in the San Diego zoo.

The Anza-Borrego Desert State Park comprises nearly half a million acres of wild, untamed desert. Flash floods, erosion and the baking heat of the sun create grotesque, twisting patterns in the dry, sandy wastes. The desert does not always have this bleak and lifeless appearance, however. In the spring, when the rains, hopefully, arrive, the floor of the desert abounds with the colors of wild flowers. The desert-growing plants illustrated here include: left Echinocactus and Grusoni Cactceae, below Ocotillo in bloom and overleaf a selection of the many species that are able to survive in these unlikely conditions.

Storm clouds above and left bring their promise of welcome rainfall to the Anza-Borrego Desert State Park. Most desert plants have a very shallow root system simply because there is no moisture deep down in the earth and the roots rely on the rainfall that penetrates only a little distance under the floor of the desert.

Typical of most people's idea of the plant is Englemann's Hedgehog Cactus right. The Ocotillo below foliates during and after wet weather but as soon as the soil dries out the leaves fall, allowing moisture to remain trapped in the plant's stems.

The strangely beautiful scene overleaf was photographed in the Living Desert Reserve, near Palm Springs.

The pictures center left and bottom left were taken at the Living Desert Reserve, a 360-acre area of the Colorado Desert situated in Palm Desert, about 15 miles southeast of Palm Springs.

The remaining pictures these pages and overleaf feature the Joshua Tree National Monument, an increasingly rare desert sanctuary, lying at the edge of the low Colorado and the high Mojave deserts, covering an area of over 850 square miles. The Joshua tree top left, bottom right and overleaf is the most famous of the plants of the area and is really a giant relative of the lily family. Sometimes attaining a height well over thirty feet, the tree bears spectacular clusters of white flowers at the ends of its branches. The Joshua tree is so-named, according to folk-lore, because of its upstretched arms.

Primitive men once lived in the vicinity, in the days when there was sufficient water to support their way of life and there are old mine shafts remaining as evidence of settlement by gold prospectors.

Above: *polo being played at El Dorado Polo Club, Indian Wells, near Palm Springs. Left: Date Garden at Indian Wells, also pictured below. The picture* right *shows the Palomar Mountain District, and overleaf the Walter Annenberg Estate from the air.*

Palm Springs has fine golf courses top left and center left *that stay green all the year round, thus earning it its title 'Golf Capital of the World'. Tennis is another popular sport in Palm Springs and there are numerous courts available.*

The aerial views above and overleaf *feature the beautifully landscaped Walter Annenberg Estate.*

The Palm Springs Tramway below and right *swings at breathtaking heights between the San Jacinto Mountains. Not surprisingly, the tramway has been described as 'the eighth engineering masterpiece in the world'.*

Perched high in this mountainous terrain is Bob Hope's house below left.

In complete contrast to the Bristol Dry Lake above in San Bernadino County, spring brings its color and delicacy left to the normally arid and sun parched Lower Desert, near Indio, right.

The road below runs through the San Bernadino National Forest, near Palm Springs.

The fourth mission to be dedicated in California was Mission San Gabriel, whose beautiful cloisters are illustrated overleaf left.

Mission Inn overleaf right is justly recognized as one of the most beautiful buildings in California. It owes its origins to an adobe cottage, begun in 1875. The mission houses, among its many treasures, the St. Francis Chapel and the Garden of the Bells.

Flanking a beautiful fountain lagoon, the magnificent Dorothy Chandler Pavilion right *and the Ahmanson Theater* above *are part of the Los Angeles Music Center for the Performing Arts which is considered to be one of the world's finest cultural centers.*

The City Hall, once the tallest building in Southern California, can be seen left behind *the peacock fountain and* below *in the background of the Civic Center Mall.*

Traffic makes its way between the timeless palms and the modern buildings of Western Avenue overleaf.

People flock to the Santa Anita Park Racetrack in Arcadia these pages and overleaf, not only to watch some of the world's top horseraces, but also in the hope of seeing some of the celebrities who patronize this outstanding race course.

Its superb location, at the foot of the San Gabriel Mountains, provides magnificent mountain scenery, while the infield displays a mosaic of beautiful flowers. During the winter racing season nearly one million special Santa Anita giant pansies can be seen in peak bloom. Of international fame this 'sport of kings' has assured for the racecourse one of the richest purse distributions annually in the world.

Adjacent to the George C. Page Museum are the La Brea Tarpits above left where excavations have revealed a wealth of fossilized bones of pre-historic animals which roamed the region some 40,000 years ago. Life-size statues of some of the beasts have been constructed on the site which also contains a typical excavation pit where the bones have been left intact.

The city's many outstanding architectural designs include the new Los Angeles County Art Museum above, which is ringed by magnificent reflecting pools; the Century Plaza and Schubert Theater right; the Post Office below; the forecourt of the Bank of America, with its water fountain and exciting sculpture center left, and the Public Library below left, flanked by the Union Bank and Bonaventure Hotel.

Traffic pulses along the Harbor Freeway in downtown L.A. overleaf.

The biggest attraction in California, the charm of Disneyland *these pages and overleaf*, lies in its make-believe magic – an enchanted park where some of Walt Disney's best-loved characters are brought to life and where it is possible to explore a Peter Pan world that never grows old; pirate ships and magic castles, riverboat rides that cruise through swampy jungles and breathtaking adventures that whirl through 'liquid space' on underwater cruises to the North Pole in the Submarine Voyage. There are so many exciting things to do and see in the seven themed lands of Main Street, Adventureland, New Orleans Square, Bear Country, Frontierland, Fantasyland and Tomorrowland, with their fun-packed special entertainments, guaranteed to keep the young wide-eyed and adults spell-bound.

By night L.A.'s exciting skyline above and below left and above right *shimmers against the backdrop of a darkening sky, as lights gleam over the vast metropolis.*

The Harbor Freeway above, right and overleaf *curves around the city, leaving trails of blazing lights, while* top center *Crocker Bank towers above the gleaming fountain.*

Creating stark silhouettes as the sun sets on the horizon, Watts Towers below *stand as a unique memorial to Simon Rodia, an Italian immigrant whose dream was 'to leave something behind in his adopted country'. The towers, erected from an assortment of flotsam and jetsam, scavenged from the city, took him thirty-three years to build and were finally completed in 1954.*

The Movieland Wax Museum on these pages is a shrine to some of the greatest stars of the 'Silver Screen'. Realistically carved in life-like wax, the figures are posed in the memorable film sets that are so closely associated with these world famous actors and actresses.

Among those on view are Fred Astaire and Ginger Rogers in the Academy Award winning 'Top Hat' above left, Katharine Hepburn and Humphrey Bogart in 'African Queen' top center, Rudolph Valentino as 'The Sheik' above, Yul Brinner and Deborah Kerr in 'The King and I' above right, Julie Andrews in 'Mary Poppins' below right, and Paul Newman and Robert Redford in 'Butch Cassidy and the Sundance Kid' below.

Nearby is the Palace of Living Arts, which features wax displays from such famous paintings as 'The Last Supper' shown below left, as well as reproductions of the Venus de Milo and other statues that are on view in the Louvre in Paris.

Fabulous Malibu overleaf noted for its famous movie colony, stretches along the West Pacific Coast Highway, from the Los Angeles city line to the extreme frontier of Ventura County.

Reflecting the spirit of Old Mexico, Olvera Street *these pages* was the birthplace of the Los Angeles pueblo and is now maintained as a traffic-free Mexican market with colorful shops, stalls and cafés. Craftsmen such as glass-blowers, silversmiths and candlemakers display their merchandise in an atmosphere heavy with perfume and spices. At the open-fronted cafés visitors can enjoy authentic Mexican food – tacos and frijoles among the most popular – quickly prepared and at a low cost.

Overleaf: *Fabulous Beverly Hills with its magnificent Plaza is a mass of colorful blooms.*

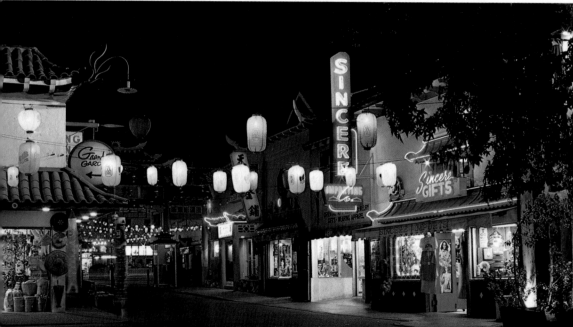

Fascinating Chinatown, created in the Eastern image above, below and center left, features picturesque pagodas above and far right ornamented with balconies and gold trim.

Sited on Hollywood Boulevard below is Mann's Chinese Theater right where the footprints and autographs of Hollywood's 'greats' are immortalized in concrete.

Farmers Market above and below *was started in 1934 by a group of independent farmers specializing in high quality produce. Today this lively market has a collection of individual shops and stalls which sell clothing, gifts and curios as well as the colorfully displayed fruit shown* above right.

L.A. constantly zings with life – by day or night – from basketball in Lafayette Park left *to a stroll along exciting Hollywood Boulevard, the main artery of the movie capital, shown* right and far right.

Marineland above and below left *is a vast oceanarium on the Pacific coast just 30 minutes south of Los Angeles, sited between Redondo Beach and San Pedro, where visitors can watch 'star' performances by 'Flipper' and his dolphin friends, performing sea-lions, 'Bubbles' the giant whale and the famous killer whales 'Orky' and 'Corky'. In the giant salt water tank huge turtles, giant bass, sharks and many exotic fish are hand-fed by a diver – watched by an audience through the tank's 170 windows.*

The Los Angeles Zoo, in Griffith Park, has an unrivalled collection of wildlife as well as the more familiar flamingoes, gorillas, elephants and Polar bears shown on these pages.
Animals are exhibited by origin, in natural habitats, in one of the world's largest bird farms, while in the fascinating Children's Zoo there is a sea-lion pool, a nursery center for newborn animals and their mothers, and a Prairie Dog Village.
The Zoo's efforts in the protection of endangered animals has earned it a high reputation for the conservation of wildlife.

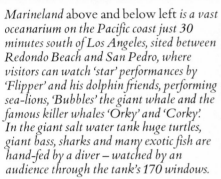

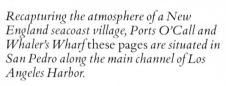

Recapturing the atmosphere of a New England seacoast village, Ports O'Call and Whaler's Wharf *these pages are* situated in San Pedro along the main channel of Los Angeles Harbor.

Fascinating stores above and center left *are filled with attractively displayed merchandise:* colonial style shops and restaurants below left, *with their quaint tavern signs and small-paned windows, line cobblestone streets, and in the harbor fishing boats, yachts and tuna clippers pass in and out in a steady stream.*

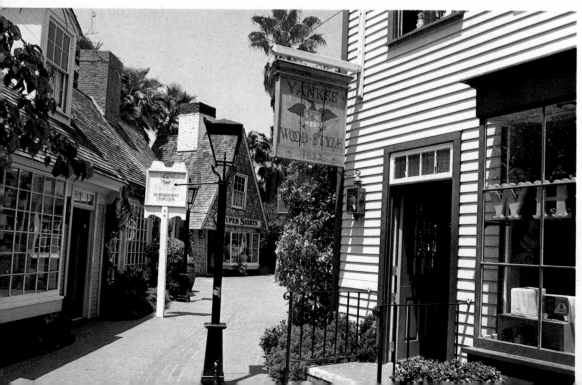

Universal City Studios featured on these
pages and overleaf *is the largest motion-
picture studio in the world, covering over 420
acres of mountainous plateau and valley.
Founded by Carl Laemmle in 1912,
Universal's early films were presented by Erich
von Stroheim, a pioneer in realistic film
direction, and some of the greatest names in
cinema history, including Deanna Durbin,
Doris Day, Rock Hudson and Tony Curtis
have been associated with the Studio's
successful films.*
*The sprawling film lot includes a variety of
sets, such as those of the wild west, a European
street built at a cost of $2 million, the shark
from 'Jaws' and a monster make-up show.*

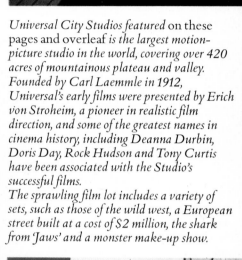

Almost two and a half million visitors are welcomed at Universal each year and the Studio provides a conducted tour of the area, aboard one of the brightly-colored Glamor-Trams, which is usually guided by an aspiring actor or actress.

Lasting about two hours, the tour takes in the entire studio and guests can see at first hand the 'behind the scenes' effects that are realistically presented on celluloid; stunt-men demonstrating their skills, a runaway tram, flash floods and a torpedo attack on one of the man-made lakes.

To end the day in this exciting arena, and perhaps catch a glimpse of one of the movie stars, visitors can head for the Sheraton-Universal deluxe hotel or the Four Stages Restaurant, which is a great place for 'making appearances'.

Sited at Long Beach, Mary's Gate Village top left *is close to the home of the 'Queen Mary', the famous retired ocean liner, which is now preserved as a museum.*

This stately ship *featured on these pages completed her final voyage on December 9, 1967 after a 14,500 mile journey that took her round South America via Cape Horn, and was purchased by the City of Long Beach at a cost of $3 million.*

The sun sets *overleaf on the splendor of the lonely coastline.*

Because of its beautiful climate, outdoor crazes come thick and fast in California... unicycles, skates and skateboards all have their turn and special facilities are provided to encourage these pursuits wherever possible.

Recreated in the style of a 1st century Roman
villa, the J. Paul Getty Museum, beautifully
illustrated on these pages, contains an
outstanding collection of Greek and Roman
antiquities, paintings and furnishings. The
design of the villa is based on the Villa dei
Papiri which was sited in the ancient city of
Herculaneum, near Pompeii, and follows the
floorplan and notes made during the 18th
century excavations. Housed in the Museum
building, the collection of antiquities includes
bronze and marble sculpture, vases and
mosaics, while the paintings collection is
representative of all major schools of Western
art from the 13th to the early 20th century.

Overleaf are shown the sculptured mountains
of Zabriskie Point in Death Valley National
Monument.

With the exception of the Amargosa Opera House at Death Valley Junction below the pictures on these pages feature Scotty's Castle, located in a desolate area of Death Valley. The Castle, with its blend of Moorish, Spanish, Italian and California Mission architecture, stands as a unique monument to Walter Scott, an early prospector, whose colorful personality has long been associated with the Valley's history. Scotty's dream was realized with the aid of his partner, millionaire Albert M. Johnson, who spared no expense in the construction and the furnishing of this unusual desert home.

Miles of undulating sand dunes cover the barren wilderness in Death Valley overleaf.

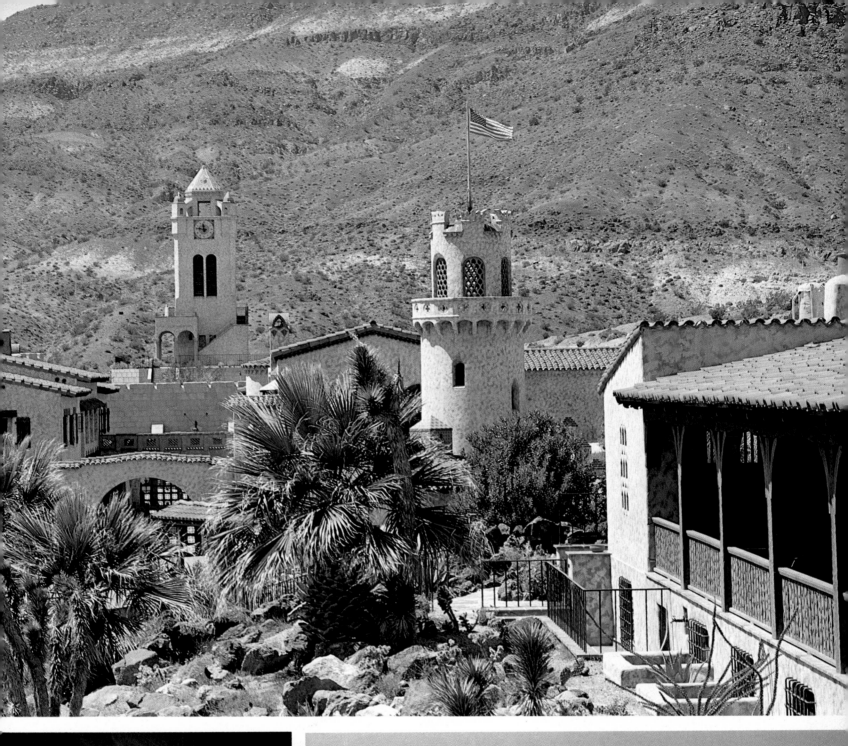

UBEHEBE CRATER

A GREAT VOLCANIC EXPLOSION SOME 3,000 YEARS AGO BLEW THIS HOLE IN THE GROUND. IT IS ABOUT 500 FEET DEEP AND ONE-HALF MILE IN DIAMETER. VOLCANIC CINDERS AND "BOMBS" WERE THROWN FOR DISTANCES UP TO FOUR MILES. THERE ARE SEVERAL SMALLER CRATERS NEARBY, SOME OF WHICH MAY NOT BE OVER 200 TO 300 YEARS OLD. UBEHEBE MEANS "BIG BASKET" IN SHOSHONE.

Awe-inspiring natural rock formations, huge craters, such as the gigantic Ubehebe Crater above and below right, and unusual desert blooms left fill the landscape in Death Valley National Monument. From Zabriskie Point above can be seen the deeply cut mudhills formed by the upheaval and erosion of an ancient lake bed, while in Devils Golf Course below and overleaf the ragged salt pinnacles cover thousands of acres in one of the hottest and lowest parts of the Valley.

Santa Barbara, retaining the rich tradition of 'Old Spain', is noted for its superb Mission overleaf left, *justly described as the "Queen of Missions", and its magnificent Court House resembling a Spanish-Moorish castle* above, above left and below.

Built in and around its historic adobes is El Paseo right, *while* left *is shown the picturesque windmill in the Danish Community of Solvang.*

Elegant Mission San Buenaventura overleaf right *was the last to be founded by Father Serra.*

Graceful and dignified, the charming old missions illustrated on these pages are part of Southern California's rich heritage. The old mission at San Juan Bautista center and above left and below is California's largest church, while below left is a further view of the mission at San Buenaventura in Ventura County. Sited on the Carmel-Monterey Peninsula is the lovely Mission of San Carlos Borromeo de Carmelo above and far right, while right can be seen the Mission of San Luis Obispo. Situated in Orange County is the Mission of San Juan Capistrano, the tranquil courtyard of which is shown overleaf.

Perched high above San Simeon, on "The Enchanted Hill", is the fabled castle and grounds of William Randolph Hearst which is now maintained as a state historical monument.

Illustrated on these pages and overleaf are some of the outstanding features of this magnificent estate: three Mediterranean style guest houses, swimming pools lined with Greek temples and superb statuary within the landscaped grounds.

On display in La Casa Grande is a splendid collection of 'Old World' treasures, including Gothic and Renaissance tapestries, Roman mosaics and fine wood carvings.

At one time the estate also contained a zoo, and today some of the imported wildlife, such as Barbary sheep, zebra and tahr goat, freely roam the hillside around "La Cuesta Encantada".

Guarding the entrance to Morro Bay is the towering 576 foot Morro Rock right, and below is shown the famous landmark of Mail Pouch Barn located on the northern outskirts of San Luis Obispo, with the San Luis Mountains rising in the background.

California's magnificent rugged coastline is particularly evident along Big Sur in Monterey County, seen above as the daytime mist hazes the horizon and above right as the setting sun casts a shimmer over the ocean's waves, while overleaf one of the world's highest highway bridges, Bixby Creek on Highway 1, arches high above the jagged shoreline.

Within the Pebble Beach area of the Monterey Peninsula the famous Pebble Beach golf course provides golfers with an exciting and challenging course, particularly at the 7th hole right.

One of the most spectacular scenic routes in Monterey is along the 17-Mile Drive which also penetrates the pine woods of the Del Monte Forest. The view left shows the Lone Cypress as the Drive curves along the rocky stretch of coast.

Pigeon Point Lighthouse, sited along the coast between Monterey and San Francisco, is shown below dramatically silhouetted against a golden sunset.

The awe-inspiring beauty of the Monterey coastline, with its craggy promontories and sheltered coves, is further exemplified in the superb photographs featured on these pages and overleaf.

Winding south along the Carmel and Big Sur coast is Highway 1, revealing the fabulous Pacific Ocean shoreline center right and the vistas in and out of the Coast Range. Shown top right is the superb scenery half a mile north of Point Sur which can be seen overleaf with lowering clouds darkening the sky as night enfolds the Point.

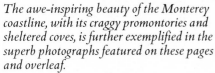

Silvery waves lap gently beneath graceful Bixby Creek Bridge seen at nightfall above, while left is shown lonely Garra Pata Creek.

Seal and Bird Rocks below right are just one of the features along famous 17-Mile Drive, and provide homes for countless shoreline birds such as cormorants and gulls, as well as for offshore herds of sea-lions and the smaller Leopard and Harbor seals. These fascinating barren rocks are a popular tourist attraction and facilities for visitors include mounted field glasses for observing the wildlife and a special picnic area.

Along the Drive's route are a wealth of skilfully designed golf courses, noted for their challenging use of ocean and forest. Revealing its particularly hazardous features is the deserted 7th hole of the Pebble Beach Golf Links below.

The pretty Victorian house shown below, built in Salinas in 1897, was once the childhood home of novelist John Steinbeck. Restored by the Valley Guild, the house is now open to the public as a gourmet luncheon restaurant.

Closely associated with the author and immortalized in his novel 'Cannery Row' are the renovated and abandoned buildings bottom left which were once thriving sardine factories in historic Monterey, which not only recalls its close links with the past as in the Pacific House center left, now maintained as a museum in the State Park, but blends the old with the new in the streamlined Convention Center top left.

Folds of rolling countryside, covered with wild flowers and dotted with trees, fill the valley surrounding Salinas above and right.

Santa Cruz, the largest of the Channel
Islands, lying across the bay from Santa
Barbara, is one of a group of islands which are
in fact small mountain tops separated from the
mainland by water. Privately owned, Santa
Cruz is a noted summer resort for the Bay
Area residents, who can explore the picturesque
island or indulge in a wide range of activities
which includes swimming, surfing and fishing.
Stretching far into the Channel's blue water is
the island's long municipal pier bottom right
and top right is shown the popular Cooper
House.

Located in Monterey County, along the south
shore of Carmel Bay, the Point Lobos State
Reserve left is an area of outstanding natural
beauty which derives its name from the
colonies of California and Stellar's sea-lions
which inhabit the offshore rocks at Punta de
los Lobos Marinos, Point of the Sea-wolves.
The reserve is an important wildlife sanctuary
and many species of land and marine life,
including pelicans, flocks of cormorants, and
otters make their homes here, free from
encroachment. From early spring until fall the
seacoast is transformed into a variegated
pattern of color as wildflowers fill the meadows
and fragrant Monterey pine woods spice the
air.

The rocky coastline along scenic 17-Mile Drive
is shown center right, and below at the aptly
named Pebble Beach, while above can be seen
the daytime view of Pigeon Point Lighthouse.

Brightly colored pumpkins, in an assortment of sizes, thickly carpet the fields right and are the obvious feature of the exciting Pumpkin Festival, seen on these pages, which is held in Half Moon Bay, San Mateo County.

A variety of events provide fun for all the family, especially for children, as they eagerly await the results of the pumpkin decoration competition, graded according to age, or have their faces gaily covered with grease paint.

All festivals attract numerous side-shows, such as the dancer below, and there are always the exotically dressed top who come to see and, most importantly, to be seen at such events.

East of San Francisco the arid area surrounding Livermore top left requires a carefully planned irrigation system to conserve essential water supplies, and the aqueduct shown above curving through the countryside provides such a need. Undulating farmland center left, furrowed in deep ridges, shows the vast acreage of cultivated land in the valley.

Huge mountain pinnacles rise to meet a cloudless sky in the Mount Diablo State Park bottom left.

Stockton, lying in the San Joaquin River Valley, is one of the largest valley cities along State 99, connected to San Francisco by a 76-mile channel which carries agricultural and manufactured goods from the Port to the San Francisco Bay Area. To the immediate west edge of downtown Stockton are the docks which serve around 700 cargo vessels a year in this fertile region with its long, warm summers. The lush valley surrounding the town is shown right flooded with warm golden tones from the sun's last rays.

Moonlight gleams over Concord below, originally founded as Todos Santos in 1868 on the Rancho Monte del Diablo, in Contra Costa County. Although initially developed as an orchard and poultry center with the introduction of the Oakland, Antioch and Eastern Railroad in 1912, the city is now mainly residential and connects with the San-Francisco-Oakland area by freeways and the Bay Area Rapid Transit System.

Without water on three sides, San Francisco
*right would possibly be just one more
conglomerate of buildings, streets and people,
but relative inaccesibility has helped to make
this place conspicuously different. Even the
most recently constructed buildings like the
Transamerica's pyramidal 'skysaver' on these
pages, reaching from the city's concrete
congestion towards an almost cloudless sky,
have their own distinctive character.*

At the heart of the city overleaf *rise the
skyscrapers of the financial district and* on
pages 152 and 153 *can be seen imposing
Union Square.*

In constructing the 20th century giants above the historical has not been altogether lost: *Alcatraz Island* left *was once the site of the most dreaded penitentiary in the U.S.,* Fort Point *below, built in 1861 to guard the Golden Gate, remains half-concealed under the south tower of the Golden Gate Bridge and* Hyde Street Pier *right gives access to historic ships.*

The Oakland Bay Bridge *overleaf links San Francisco with Oakland, its neighboring city across the water.*

*Cable cars on these pages and overleaf
right are the rolling symbols of San Francisco,
for this is the only city in the world with an
operating cable car system. Legend has it that
Andrew Hallidie, a London-born engineer,
was moved to invent the system by compassion
for the beasts that supplied the power for the
old horse cars.*

*In 1869, watching an overworked horse slip
and fall as it hauled a heavy load up one of
the city's steep slopes, he vowed to stop such
cruelty and built the Clay Street Railroad
Company. Since then the design has not
changed…the cars still have no engines, but
are hoisted along by means of a steel cable
permanently moving at a speed of 9½ miles an
hour.*

*Between manicured hedges and blossoming
hydrangeas, Lombard pages 162/163, the
most picturesque of San Francisco's streets,
winds tortuously downhill between
Leavenworth and Hyde.*

Sailing is a popular form of relaxation for city-dwellers and Marina District left and overleaf provides moorings within easy access of the city center. At the western end of the district the Palace of Fine Arts above right rises like an ornate bubble.

The Renaissance architecture of the City Hall above, home to the city's board of supervisors, is frequently referred to as a classically extravagant contrast to the ultra-modern design of many of the San Francisco buildings, among them the Embarcadero Center right, which has added high-rise office buildings, shops and restaurants to the Financial Center or the Hallidie Plaza below where weary shoppers can pause for a while.

In the Embarcadero Plaza below right, Vaillancourt's controversial sculpture composed of 101 concrete blocks points the way to the clock tower of the old Ferry Building, a reminder of the days when ferry boats carried traffic across the bay.

Intended to resemble a firehose nozzle, Coit Tower on Telegraph Hill, rises beyond Fisherman's Wharf pages 168/169.

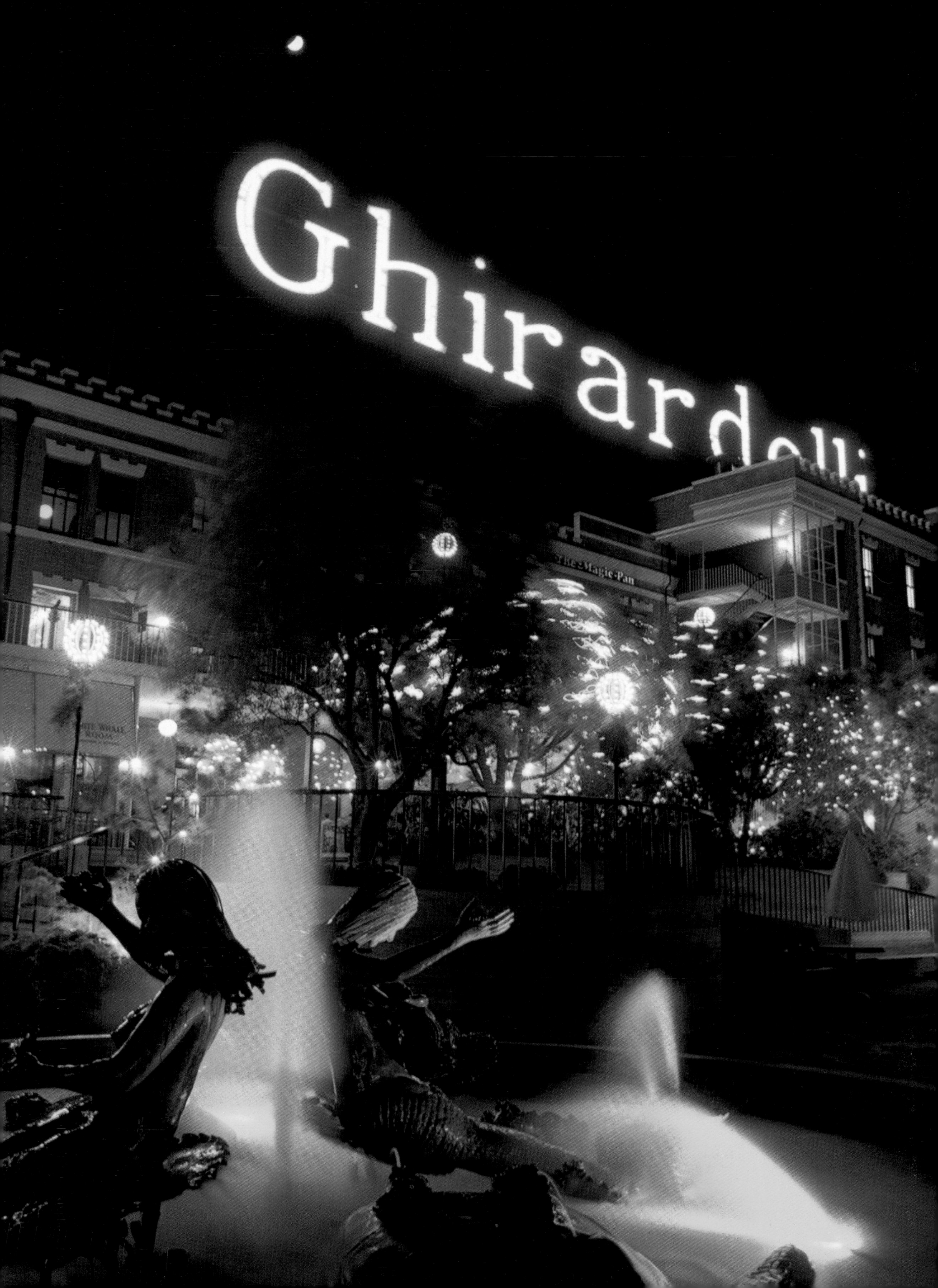
Ghirardelli
The Magic Pan

In Ghirardelli Square left *is the whimsical mermaid fountain* overleaf left, *designed by Ruth Asawa, and which forms the focal point of this famous square.*

Fisherman's Wharf on this page *is the embarking and landing point of San Francisco's many fishermen. Picturesque, and in some respects bizarre, it is world-renowned for its fine sea food.*

In the Golden Gate Park, a beautiful stretch of parkland wrested from what was once a wasteland of rolling dunes, are the bronze Buddha overleaf right *which looks benevolently upon the people of San Francisco; the Japanese Tea Garden* page 175 *where clear pools reflect, with exotic artistry, the dwarf trees that line their banks, and the Victorian Conservatory* page 174 *with its outstanding collection of flora.*

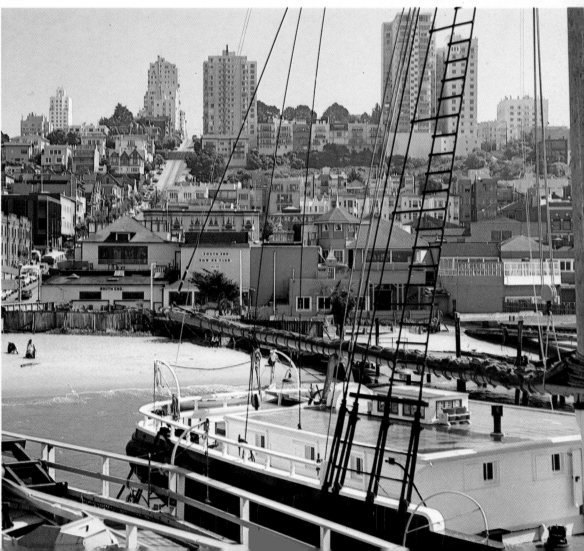

The precipitous slopes of San Francisco's hillside streets these pages, *where the stacked rooftops stairstep up the hills* pages 180/181, *afford magnificent views of the city and the bay beyond, and a ride in a cable car* overleaf *is an ideal alternative to an arduous climb on foot.*

Stanford University center left, founded in 1883 by railroad baron Leland Stanford and his wife in memory of their son, encompasses 8,200 acres. The Memorial Church above left *and* below left, *with its exquisite Venetian mosaics and stained glass windows* overleaf, *lies at the heart of the campus in a quadrangle of sandstone buildings.*

The University of California in Berkeley above *and* far right *and its famous campanile are set in a strikingly attractive campus amid undulating hills. The fine work on the ceiling of the main library* right *is particularly beautiful.*

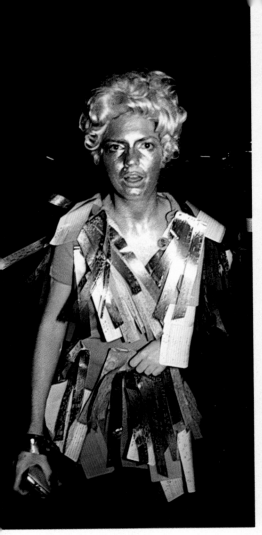

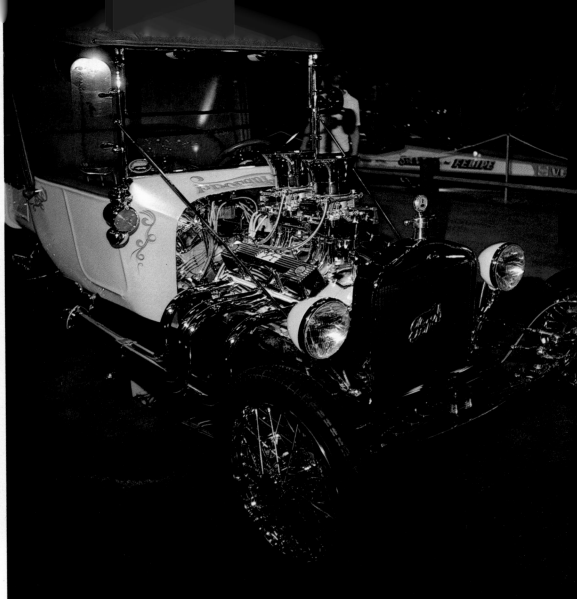

Outdoor murals like those left by Mujeres
Muralistas, three women artists, brighten
walls and fences in the Mission District.

Extravagant costumes above and below are
an essential feature of a Hooker's Ball in Cow
Palace and, also on display in Cow Palace,
turbo charged engines and polished vintage
cars below right and above right reflect the
skill and care of a bygone era.

San Francisco's famous Barbary Coast is
shown overleaf with the dark water of the
bay lit by myriad lights.

Spanning the historic Golden Gate of San Francisco, the Golden Gate Bridge on these pages, and overleaf *shrouded in the low-hanging cloud of a San Francisco morning, is the tallest and largest single span suspension bridge in the world. In defiance of the inconsistencies of the elements a 90 ft. wide traffic deck and two pedestrian walks are miraculously suspended above the ever-shifting moods of the waters below.*

Oakland Bay Bridge on these pages and overleaf is the world's largest steel bridge, jointed in midbay at Yerba Buena Island by a tunnel of enormous dimensions. At night what is really a superbly dovetailed pattern of bridges glimmers with a thousand lights against the most spectacular sunsets.

The distinctive outline of San Francisco below right stands silhouetted against a brilliantly colored evening sky.

Many objections were raised to the initial building of the Golden Gate Bridge on these pages. "The Golden Gate is one of nature's perfect pictures… let us not disfigure it", wrote one of San Francisco's newspapers in 1930. Yet, apart from its more practical functions, the bridge has proved to have an air of mystique and poetry of its own which has made it one of the city's most famous symbols.

As night falls on the Oakland Bay Bridge overleaf, the traquil waters reflect the glow from the glittering lights along the shoreline.

Beneath the Golden Gate Bridge the rugged rocks and sparkling waters of the San Francisco Bay provide an ideal resort for seals and surfers alike. To the people who live on its shores the bay is an expanse of water to be cherished, protected and above all, enjoyed.

A magnificent aerial view of Oakland Bay Bridge is pictured overleaf, and on pages 206/207 the dizzy vantage point of Twin Peaks provides a breathtaking view of Market Street and downtown San Francisco.

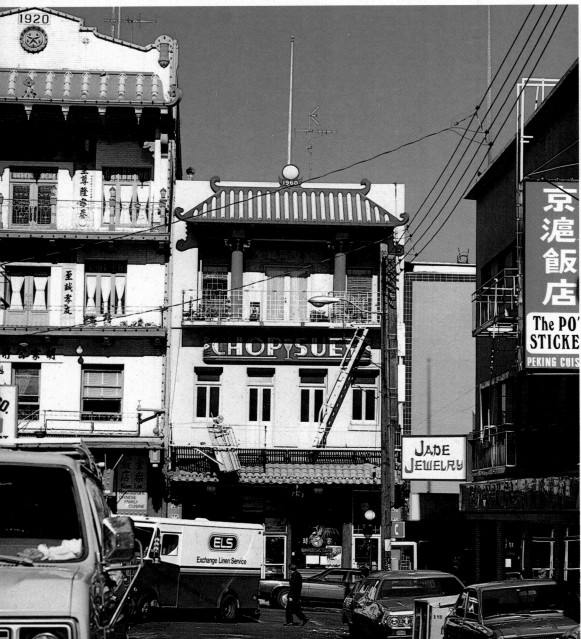

The original Chinatown these pages and overleaf, built up around Grant Avenue, was destroyed in the devastating fire of 1906 but was subsequently rebuilt and today this neighborhood with its distinctive architecture and customs still provides a fascinating glimpe of the Orient transplanted, albeit with some concessions made to the American way of life.

Although a poor imitation of the original Barbary Coast which emerged in the days of the original California 'Gold Rush', with its blazing lights, bars, clubs and restaurants these pages it still attracts innumerable visitors who flock to the city that introduced 'topless' entertainment to America.

The gabled houses of Steiner Street overleaf stand outlined against the high rise blocks of modern San Francisco, and on pages 216/217 Edith Coolbirth Park provides a panoramic view of the city by night.

AMATEUR TOPLESS

ROARING 20'S

ROARING 20'S

ROARING 20's
Accepts
ALL MAJOR
CREDIT CARDS

LIVE ACTS

IT'S DYNAMITE!

LIVE STAGE

SEX CIRCUS

GARDEN OF

CLOSED

OFF BROADWAY

EXOTIC LADY WR

The Napa Valley lies just north of San Francisco and is considered to be synonymous with 'The Wine Country'. The area is ideal for the growing of fine grapes and there are some 22,000 acres under cultivation.
Europeans, with their long tradition of wine making, came to the area in the 19th century and established their vineyards and cellars. The ideal time to visit Napa Valley is in the fall when not only the lovely countryside can be enjoyed in all the tranquility that this time of the year brings, but there is also the liveliness and bustle of the grape harvest.

Architecture in the wine growing region varies from traditional *left,* Gothic *top right, center right and below,* to Greco-Californian *bottom right.*

The long history of wine making in Napa Valley is recorded in the colorful stained glass panel above in Sebastiana Vineyards, where the view top left was also photographed.

The huge casks left which seem to stretch for miles are in the Christian Brothers' winery and the smiling gentleman below is Hans Kornell of the Hans Kornell Champagne Cellars.

The modernity of the champagne vats below left brings a touch of the 20th century to a time-honored process.

Casks above are piled high in Hacienda Winery, noted, in addition to its fine wines, as being the place 'where it all began'. The first European wine grapes were planted here in 1862 by the Hungarian nobleman Count Agoston Haraszthy.

Sterling vineyards, in whose buildings the picture right was taken, acquired their first vineyard property in 1964 but they are already one of the largest of the small wineries in the Napa Valley.

There is much to see and do in the Napa and Sonoma Valleys besides visiting the wine growing areas. Much of California's colorful past is to be seen, particularly, in Sonoma, whose City Hall is shown top left. Also in Sonoma is the Toscano Hotel, the annexe of which is pictured top, and the Mission San Francisco Solano above which dates from 1832.

The Bale Grist Mill bottom left is in the State Historic Park in Napa Valley and below is shown the Cheese Factory in Sonoma.

The Silverado Golf Club right and above right provides facilities for both recreation and competition, and its graceful Club House is pictured center left.

The Marin County Shore, stretching from Point Reyes to the Golden Gate, is a paradise for shorebound visitors who can enjoy rock fishing, hang-gliding, clamming and, for the hardy, swimming in its shallow bays. Wide, sandy beaches, such as those of Dillon below right and Drake's below slope down to choppy, azure waters and above is shown beautiful Drake's Bay, where, it is said, Sir Francis Drake first landed his ship, the 'Golden Hind'.

Magnificent Point Reyes, from Chimney Rock, can be seen overleaf, its beaches above right pounded by foaming surf, while left is pictured the Point Reyes Lighthouse, overlooking the reefs from its vantage point high on the rocky coastline.

Called by Mark Twain "one of the strangest freaks of nature", Mono Lake above left, at the northern end of the Mammoth area near Lee Vining, is bordered by a fantastic 'moonscape' of delicate tufa formation rising from the old lake bed.

Crags and spires, once the remains of a volcanic mountain, rise in jagged peaks to 1,200 feet from the canyon floor in Pinnacles National Monument above.

Bridgeport, once known as 'Big Meadow', is set in a wide, fertile valley in Mono County. Its famed, classically designed Courthouse below was constructed from hand-quarried local granite in 1880, and is one of the oldest courthouses still in use in America.

Snow capped peaks dwarf the dusty Sonora Pass, in Mono County left, and right is shown the tranquil San Luis Reservoir.

In a state of arrested decay, in what is now a State Historic Park, the buildings of Bodie these pages stand as mute reminders of this, once one of the most raucous and booming gold mining towns of the West. Bodie was a boom town in the mid-nineteenth century and at the peak of its notoriety it supported 65 saloons and there was an average of one murder each day.

The road to the town of Bodie passes Mono Lake overleaf, east of the Sierra.

The countless visitors who come to enjoy the beauty and variety that the Yosemite National Park these pages has to offer owe a great debt to the dedication of an amateur naturalist, John Muir. Strangely enough, Muir was not born in America. He was a native of Scotland and, although he emigrated to Wisconsin as a boy, he traveled a great deal before finally settling down in California. From 1868 to 1873 Muir lived in Yosemite and fell in love with its magic. He made valuable contributions and observations in geology and glaciology, and developed a passionate interest in conservation, culminating in his involvement in the establishment of the National Park System. Muir died in 1914 but he at least saw his dream realized; the preservation and conservation of his beloved Yosemite.

The icy waters of McKay Creek are shown overleaf on Sonora Pass in Sierra Nevada.

High in the Sierra Nevada is Silver Lake *top left.*

Yosemite National Park comprises almost 1,200 square miles of breathtaking beauty. It was created, principally, when huge blocks of granite, formed beneath the earth's surface, buckled and lifted. Glacial action, of a more recent date, continued nature's handiwork by carving huge valleys and creating lakes. Waterfalls tumble down granite rock faces and the peaks are sculpted into fantastic and beautiful shapes. Wildflowers and wild life abound in the area's many acres of pine, fir and oak forest.

The Merced River *right threads its way along the floor of the Yosemite Valley passing, on its way, such towering cliffs as El Capitan* below *and the mist-shrouded and mysterious Cathedral Spires* left.

Autumn colors the leaves in the Yosemite National Park *above and winter's snow lends its own special magic to the banks of the Dana River* overleaf.

Tranquil lakes – a fisherman's paradise –
majestic, towering cliffs and peaks, lofty
waterfalls adding their grandeur and their
music, dense forests, an abundance of wildlife
of all kinds and the knowledge that here is a
monumental work of nature; the Yosemite
National Park is all this and more. Within
certain periods camping is allowed and hiking
and climbing are equally popular pursuits.
Both saddle and pack animals may be rented
and there is always a heavy demand for
horseback riding facilities. With such an
abundance of water, swimming may be enjoyed
but, with safety in mind, this is not permitted
near waterfalls or in swift rivers. The view
overleaf is a clear indication of why this is so!
From about mid-December facilities for skiing
are available; there are more than fifty miles of
cross-country ski and snowshoe trails
maintained by the National Park Service.

The Yosemite National Park is well provided
with restaurants, cafeterias, lodges, hotels and
cabins for the use of the countless visitors who
come to take advantage of the sights afforded
by this scenic wonderland.

Tahoe is California's major ski center and the lake is a veritable recreational mecca. It measures some 22 miles north to south and 12 miles west to east and has a 71 mile shoreline drive. The lake takes its name from the Washo Indian word meaning 'lake'. The waters of the lake are particularly noted for their clarity and depth.

Along Lake Tahoe's south shore, which is more heavily populated than the north shore, there are resorts, private cabins, motels and public beaches. South Lake Tahoe, on the California-Nevada border, is the area's major city.

Emerald Bay top left is one of Lake Tahoe's most famous scenic attractions and its waters surround Emerald Isle, the lake's only island.

Many years ago there was a vast forest of
Sequoia sempervirens – the coast redwood –
the world's tallest tree, in an area stretching
from the Santa Lucia Mountains right down
to Oregon. Most of the giants that remain are
to be found along Highway 101 between
Leggett and Crescent City. For a small fee it is
still possible to drive a car through one of the
trees on this Avenue of the Giants above.

The huge, timber railway bridge top right is
at Fort Bragg, the largest city on the coast
between San Francisco and Eureka.

The mouth of Russian River is the setting for
the peaceful scene left.

Almost lost in the mist below is Zanotti's
dairy, near Orick, on Highway 101, the
gateway to the Redwood National Park.

The coastal scene center right was taken from
Highway 1, north of Westport, and the hills
below right were pictured in Mendocino
County.

Striking examples of volcanic activity are
shown overleaf; the aptly-named Chaos
Crags, in Lassen Volcanic National Park.

In 1914 Lassen Peak started to erupt, culminating, in 1915, in a massive release of vapor, ashes and lava. Eruptions continued, though on a decreasing scale, until 1917. The visitor to the area above can today, therefore, see evidence of the immense power of nature both past and present.

The beauty of nature's work at a headland north of Russian Gulch top left contrasts effectively with the work of man in the Shasta Dam center left, in Mendocino Main Street bottom left and, particularly, in the abandoned mine below.

Rising out of the evergreen forest right are the granite crags of Castle Crags State Park and overleaf is pictured the serenity of Clear Lake, the largest lake wholly in California.

The immensity of the fallen giant in Calaveras Big Trees State Park is amply demonstrated on page 256.

First published in Great Britain 1979 by Colour Library International Ltd.
© Illustrations: Colour Library International Ltd., 163 East 64th St., New York, N.Y. 10021.
Colour separations by La Cromolito, Milan, Italy.
Display and text filmsetting by Focus Photoset, London, England.
Printed and bound by SAGDOS - Brugherio (MI), Italy.
ISBN 0-8317-1150-7 Library of Congress Catalogue Card No. 79-7593
Published in the United States of America by Mayflower Books, Inc., New York City
Published in Canada by Wm. Collins and Sons, Toronto